Our Sweet Little Time

A YEAR IN HAIKU

Hamish Ironside

With illustrations by
BARNABY RICHARDS

Published in 2009 by IRON Press,
5 Marden Terrace, Cullercoats, North Shields,
Northumberland, NE30 4PD, UK
Telephone: +44 (0)191 253 1901
Email: ironpress@blueyonder.co.uk
www.ironpress.co.uk

ISBN 978-0-9552450-7-7

Printed in the UK by TJ International,
Padstow, on FSC-certified 80gsm
Munken Premium paper

Mixed Sources
Product group from well-managed
forests and other controlled sources
www.fsc.org Cert no. SGS-COC-2482
© 1996 Forest Stewardship Council
FSC

Typeset in Walbaum and Gill Sans

IRON Press books are distributed by Central Books
and represented by Inpress Limited, Collingwood Buildings,
38 Collingwood Street, Newcastle upon Tyne, NE1 1JF
Telephone: +44 (0)191 229 9555
www.inpressbooks.co.uk

*for Julia
and Aspen*

Contents

Acknowledgements

My thanks are due to the editors of the following publications, in which some of the poems first appeared: *Acorn*, *Blithe Spirit*, *Frogpond*, *Mayfly*, *Modern Haiku* and *Presence*.

Thanks to Barnaby Richards for his illustrations; to Michael Fell, Julia Ironside, Kate Jones and Matthew Paul for advice and encouragement; to Fabian Ironside for his very thoroughgoing critique, which did more than anything else to help give shape to the book; and to Pete Mortimer for being as supportive an editor as a writer could wish for.

'I ask: what am I doing here?
And, at once, this *I*
Becomes unreal.'

DAG HAMMARSKJÖLD
(*tr. Leif Sjöberg and W. H. Auden*)

'After returning from midwest
Went to my home 2 Hill Place
God organized all the rest
We did not plummet into space.'

ERNEST NOYES BROOKINGS

woken from dreams
of an old girlfriend
by my fiancée

daydreams of sex
segue into memories
of sharpening a chisel

running past
a strip of trees
a strobe of sun

morning rain—
crow drops down
like a bust umbrella

rusty nails and washers
swept into a corner—
low tide

slow walk from home
to the church—
rain resting on leaves

bar-room jazz—
my wife plays along
on the back of my neck

this vast sunset
diminishing and enlarging
this vast snowscape

fingers of memory
groping after a word—
Northern Lights

river flood—
trees
up to their knees

travelling in fog—
the curve of a fence
tends to infinity

hawthorn flowers—
my father shows me
what I miss by running

after the interview
I watch the big pink sun
die out

winter dusk—
the sound of knives sharpening
from a nearby tree

mimosa leaves—
a childhood lampshade
is unforgotten

getting to know
the community   walking around
the cemetery

winterspring—
I shake the snow
off daffodils' heads

sun picks up
hailstones at rest
on the melting lake

at the book fair
Darth Vader
gets in everyone's way

hazy sundown—
hedgerows silhouetted
in ranks of grey

words fly across a screen
to teach me to type:
futility . . . *hopeless* . . . *humiliation* . . .

I find the pretty path
along the canal
only after quitting

five years on
the fallen yew
flourishes

Easter Sunday—
obscure hymns show us up
as dilettantes

evening drizzle—
cherry blossom
stuck to cars

wedding reception—
a balloon on the ceiling
swaying drunkenly

a gangly heron
disperses itself
in its treetop

with such soft needles
the larch becomes
a conifer again

I run in the alley
as others run out—
pear drop smell of graffiti

yearfuls of coins
found on the ground
pay the meanest debt

the elderly poet
checks the pulse
of his favourite rose

still in his suit
desultorily
a man tries his rake

midnight—
the slow clops
of a police horse

Sunday evening—
unfinished poem
like a running sore

the zoo from outside:
the ostrich on the bare patch
where he goes to hide

sun and wind—
the frisbee tilt
of a seagull

yesterday's sun
cooled by rain
within my skin

calm evening—
my tired mind
browsing through itself

skyline of scaffolding
silhouettes of cranes
the city is never finished

in the street
a giant panda lifts its head
for a smoke

even in hiding
the full moon
teaches us a lesson

faded crisp packets
by the railway . . .
all the rooms I've lived in

Sunday afternoon—
a wasp, stuck
at a wide open window

fondly I scrutinize
the mosquito
after beating it to death

we pick our way around snails
in the garden
of a house we can't afford

parenting class—
my attention wanders
to distant thunder

brown clouds
in the sky; in the river
brown clouds

coming off the phone
my wife informs me
that I was never breastfed

our neighbour invites us
to admire the invitation
to a party we're not invited to

after the grievances
finding words
for the birthday card

at the doctor's
her heartbeat crackling
like the moon landing

in the charity shop
a Clanger and I
gaze at each other

thick salt air—
a gull at the river's edge
contemplates half a fish

we leave hospital
empty-handed—
freaky moon

drinking tea like it's beer,
beer like it's tea . . .
laborious vigil

leaving the Barbican
a man's deformed head
becomes folk art

as they laugh
the raconteur
wipes his knife

madonna and child gazing
at the sunny square
from a dim window

making toy scissors
of the surgeon's knife
I cut her loose to life

lindens in the breeze
through a hospital window—
all the time in the world

watching her dreaming
at three days old—softly, news
breaks through the door

returning to the river
after the birth—
the dead tree fallen

rainy afternoon—
ducks tucked up in sleep
floating downriver

my wife bites
our daughter's nails
as I bite my own

babyless belly . . .
the cheap thrill
of my wife as a stranger

even if I run
I hear my daughter crying
in a dog's bark

a dream of parrots
a dream of Armageddon—
my mind a spinning coin

a sense of bad faith—
wishing for nothing
better than sleep

just a few brown leaves
on the plane tree; just a few
grey hairs in my sideburns

rushing out early—
sun through sleepy eyes
dreamily overlucent

silver birch saplings
in the hospital garden
bone-white, bone-thin

stroking
a stunned wren—
as though for her sake

at the end of the day
I see the flowers
that were there all along

arguing at night—
a glance at condoms
bought in the morning

summer morning—
warm breath of shrubbery
where the path lies low

sliding the pole up,
a brief equilibrium—
the hang of the punt

summer's end—
an ice cream van
reeking of burgers

in my address book,
ruled out: those I cared for least,
those I cared for most

contemplating writing
my diary; contemplating
burning my diaries

daydreams of solar panels
as the sun goes down
as the train sits still

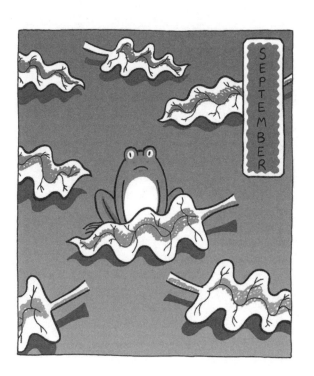

base of a plane tree
wrapped round a gravestone;
candlewax on a bottle

sometimes the leaf
you think is a frog
is a frog

dragonflies
in wet air . . . shapes
of swimming snakes

a sunflower watches
a man sweeping up
the year's first leaf-fall

autumn twilight . . .
the moon brings itself
into focus

the solipsism
of the long-distance runner—
the mind—world prism

in my daughter's eye
my own eye
looking back at me

allotments at dawn—
patches of slumped mist
like sleeping tramps

after everything—
the cactus withering
for want of neglect

hoarse indignation
of the bear with the bucket:
'. . . term'ly ill *chil*dren . . .'

heart skipping
a beat, flipping
like a landed fish

walking out alone
to the river at midnight—
a room of my own

syncopated scrunch
of father and son running
on the gritty path

a strand of sycamore
dangling through a roof—
a hand trailing out of bed

estate agent's grin
lurking in the hall, ready
to take people in

mist burning off—
a skyscape sketches itself
over a morning

abject loneliness . . .
seeing it in someone else
I sometimes miss it

we watch the weather
scrape its grey belly
over a jagged ridge

tarn at dusk—
beech leaves
lapping the shore

when the time comes
my halting diary
claims its third pen

crows at twilight—
scraps of charred paper
escaping a bonfire

a tramp hard at it—
can of K in one hand,
he talks to the other

as the drink sinks in
so the capitulation
to certainty

that time of day:
is that the sun or moon?
that time of year

in a cold phone box
my wife's sadness
muffled by traffic

moonlit in black water
the heron's mastery
of solitude

we laugh together
until I realise
she's crying

my daughter's screaming
settled by footage
of war in Iraq

my hands know things I don't—
words I can spell
only by writing

forty-one geese
by a long jump pit—
autumn morning

I berate my friends—
then when my wife joins in
I defend them

hotel transience
forging the illusion
of permanence somewhere

the one leaf
in a winter tree
is a parrot

the cloud of oil
gone up in smoke:
the city's flagrant wig

in freezing water
a duck mounts a duck
with little ceremony

a thrown coin—
the blind accordionist
affects not to hear

plasterers smoke like squaddies,
fold dust sheets together
like mother and daughter

as one lands, one flits
to the branch where the next sits—
a wheel of blue tits

winter afternoon—
snow, sun and cloud play
scissors, paper, stone

early morning rain—
a man tells a boy
about insurance